WORLD INSIDERS

AUTHENTIC VIDEOS FROM *INSIDER*

Kuniko Yoshida   Anthony Allan

KINSEIDO

Kinseido Publishing Co., Ltd.

3-21 Kanda Jimbo-cho, Chiyoda-ku,

Tokyo 101-0051, Japan

First published 2021 by Kinseido Publishing Co., Ltd.

Cover design   Takayuki Minegishi

Videos   From Business Insider. © 2021 Insider Inc.. All rights reserved.
              ※映像の詳細は巻末を参照

音声ファイル無料ダウンロード

http://www.kinsei-do.co.jp/download/4121

この教科書で ⬇ DL 00 の表示がある箇所の音声は、上記 URL または QR コードにて無料でダウンロードできます。自習用音声としてご活用ください。

▶ PC からのダウンロードをお勧めします。スマートフォンなどでダウンロードされる場合は、**ダウンロード前に「解凍アプリ」をインストール**してください。

▶ URL は、**検索ボックスではなくアドレスバー (URL 表示欄)** に入力してください。

▶ お使いのネットワーク環境によっては、ダウンロードできない場合があります。

◉ CD 00   左記の表示がある箇所の音声は、教室用 CD (Class Audio CD) に収録されています。

WORLD INSIDERS
PREFACE

　本書はニュースウェブサイトの　INSIDER のコンテンツから選りすぐった 14 本のビデオの内容を学び、発展的な語学練習を行うために編纂したものです。INSIDER（www.insider.com）は、Business Insider 社が 2009 年に設立し、2020 年現在、14 か国でインターナショナルエディションが展開されています。報道されるニュースは、政治、社会問題、健康、科学、文化、生活、環境問題等の幅広いジャンルにわたっており、まさに"今"を伝えるメディアのひとつになっています。

　本書では、このメディアを利用してリスニングからリーディング、ライティングからスピーキング、へと段階を追って学習していきます。全 14 ユニットは、**Warm-Up, Video-Viewing 1, Video Viewing 2, Reading, Writing, Speaking and Discussion** の 6 種類のタスクで構成されています。各タスクの特徴は次の通りです。

Warm-Up

映像を見る前に特定のシーンの静止画を見て、映像の内容を予測します。映像の要点をあらかじめ知るとともに、未知の単語が質問文にある場合は、それを調べて理解が容易になるよう準備をすることがねらいです。

Video-Viewing 1

映像を見て、全体の大まかな展開をつかみます。詳細にこだわることなく、概要を理解することがねらいです。

Video-Viewing 2

Video-Viewing 1 で見た流れに沿って、各パートの詳細を聴き取っていきます。大事な情報が含まれる部分に絞っていますので、正確に聴き取って、映像全体の理解を深めることがねらいです。

Reading

ビデオに関連した 350 ワード程度の文章を読んで、内容理解のための質問に答えます。文章は全編書き下ろしで、構文は EFL 学習者にとって理解しやすいものとなっており、ワードレベルも 4000 語レベルを基準としています。当

該トピックを深く理解するのに最適な内容で、流れに沿って質問に答える中で、トピックに関連する付加情報を得ることをねらいとしています。

Writing

各ユニットに関連した内容で、提示された状況に沿って、Useful Expressions を使いながら、自分の考えを表現します。どのユニットでも各自が思った内容を表現できるような工夫がなされています。メール形式の短い文章で考えを英語で表現することをねらいとしています。

Speaking and Discussion

各ユニットの仕上げとして、与えられた会話の続きを Useful Expressions を使ってペアで考えて発話します。会話の方向性はある程度絞られますが、比較的自由に内容を考えて英語を使って意見を交換することがねらいです。

　本書が英語学習に役立つと同時に、世界へ目を向けるきっかけになってくれるよう願っています。最後になりましたが、本書の作成にあたり金星堂の長島吉成氏に多大なるご協力とご支援を賜りました。ここに謝意を表します。

吉田国子

Anthony Allan

WORLD INSIDERS CONTENTS

UNIT 1
Don't Sneeze on Me!

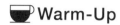 Warm-Up

映像の写真をヒントに内容を予測して、次の質問に英語で答えましょう。

1. **35 M/S**
How fast do you think is an ordinary person's sneeze?

....

....

2. How many people will you probably affect if you show symptoms of the flu?

....

....

 Video-Viewing 1

 online video    online audio

 DL 02   ⊙ CD 1-02

ビデオを見て、各キーワードを映像が出てくる順序に並べた場合、空所に入るものを a〜e から選んでみましょう（1つ不要な選択肢があります）。

(^{1})
↓
(^{2})
↓
The direction a germ-infected gas cloud moves
↓
(^{3})
↓
(^{4})
↓
What you should do when you feel sick

- **a.** Danger zones around you
- **b.** How far germ-infected droplets can travel in the air
- **c.** How fast a germ-infected cloud made by your sneeze can travel
- **d.** How the infection spreads
- **e.** Possible preventing measures in the crowded place.

▶️ Video-Viewing 2

以下は映像の内容をまとめたものです。
空所に適語を入れましょう。

🎧 DL 02　💿 CD 1-02

How a germ-infected cloud and droplets travel

Speed	Distance	Direction
Cloud: at up to _____ per second	**Droplets**: up to _____ to _____	**Cloud**: rises _____

Facts about the flu virus

The flu virus
- can spread through a room in _____.
- remain suspended in the air for up to _____.

How the flu virus can spread (in an office of 100 desks)

MON.→→→→→→TUE.→→→→→→→→→→→→→→→→→→→→→SUN. / MON.→→→→→→→→→→→→→→→→→→→→→FRI.		
Only you are infected.	_____ people around you are infected but show no _____.	Virus potentially infects another _____ people around the 1~2 people infected earlier × the number of days	_____ sick people = over _____ %

📖 Reading

次の文を読んで、あとの問いに答えましょう。　🎧 DL 03　💿 CD 1-03 ～ 💿 CD 1-07

online audio

An Egg and a Trick

For the majority of people, the egg is a simple source of food that has great versatility. Unlike many other types of food, it can be found on plates around the planet during breakfast, lunch and dinner. However, for certain scientists, the egg is much more than just a source of easy-to-utilize nourishment—it represents an
5　important tool for fighting viruses.

In any discussion on viruses, it is important to understand three key words and how they are related. "Pathogens" are micro-organisms that can infect the body and cause diseases. On the surface of each pathogen there are "antigens," which alert the body that an infection has occurred. In response, our body's immune system
10　produces "antibodies" to fight the unwanted viral invasion.

In order to generate a vaccine for a particular virus, scientists must first generate the antigen itself in a laboratory. This is done using cells, including those in the

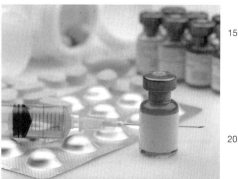

embryos inside chicken eggs. The second stage involves taking the antigen from the cells and removing any parts of the egg the antigen grew in. Then the antigen is completely isolated and purified to produce the final product, the all-important vaccine.

15

Vaccines actually play a clever trick to protect our body. When we receive an injection, the vaccine works by mimicking

20

the pathogens causing the disease. In other words, the vaccine pretends to be the same pathogen but isn't. To the body's immune system, it seems to be a virus or bacteria when in actual fact, the vaccine is a friendly substance. And because of this deception, our immune system is stimulated into action by quickly building up antibodies to counter the potentially dangerous pathogens.

25

Each time we receive a vaccination for a particular virus, our body's immune system remembers the pathogen that caused the infection. Then, if the same pathogen invades our body again, our immune system is able to respond even faster and with more strength. This is because it creates a much larger number of antibodies the second time around.

30

(334 words)

1. Which of the following protects you from getting sick?
   a. antigens
   b. antibodies
   c. embryos
   d. pathogens

2. What critical role does a vaccine play in our body?
   a. attacking antibodies
   b. building up antigens
   c. mimicking pathogens
   d. stimulating pathogens

3. When and how is a chicken egg used in the process of making a vaccine?

_____

_____

4. What happens in our bodies when we receive a vaccination against an infection?

_____

_____

5. What difference can we see in our immune system between the first encounter with pathogens and a second encounter?

_____

_____

✍ Writing

台湾の友人 Yu-En に、自国の感染症対策について聞いてみたいと思っています。考えられる対策を 3 つ挙げて、それらを実施したかどうか尋ねるメールを完成させましょう。

(聞きたい感染症対策)

1. [　　　　　　　]　　**2.** [　　　　　　　]　　**3.** [　　　　　　　]

Dear Yu-En,

In the news, I heard that your country succeeded in stopping the pandemic outbreak of an infectious disease. So, I'm really curious about how your country did it successfully. Did the government take any strong measures such as _____ ? Did the people do anything special as well? And can you tell me about _____ ? Also, I'd like to know if _____

_____ .

☞ Useful Expressions「興味を持っている、と言うときの表現」

I'm interested in ... / I'm curious about ... / Can you tell me about ...?
I wish I knew more about ... / I'd love to know ...

📢 Speaking and Discussion 🎧 DL 04 💿 CD 1-08

次の Aki と Bob の会話を聞いて内容を理解しましょう。その後ペアを組み、各自 Aki
と Bob になって Useful Expressions を参考に、会話の続きをつくってみましょう。

Bob: Aki, something annoying happened on the packed train this morning.

Aki: What happened? Did you lose your wallet or something?

Bob: No, a man standing by me kept coughing without taking any preventative measures.

Aki: Wasn't he wearing a mask?

Bob: Nope. And he never covered his mouth or tried not to cough.

Aki: Well, didn't you say anything to him?

· · · · · · · · · · · · · · ↓続き↓ · · · · · · · · · · · · · · · · · · ·

Bob: Yes, I did. I said, "_____."

Aki: Then?

Bob: He said nothing, so I told him, "_____

_____."

Aki: _____.

👉 Useful Expressions

「不快なことを伝える、苦情を言うときの表現」

I'm sorry to say this, but … / Can you do anything about …?
I'm annoyed/angry about … / If I were you, …. / Unless…, I will….

UNIT 2
Hard-Working Dads

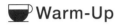Warm-Up

映像の写真をヒントに内容を予測して、次の質問に英語で答えましょう。

1.  Why does the male hardhead catfish hold the eggs in his mouth?

....

....

2. Why does the male reha bird have to raise multiple families at once?

....

....

▶️📷 Video-Viewing 1

online / video   online / audio

DL 05   CD 1-09

ビデオを見て、各キーワードを映像が出てくる順序に並べた場合、空所に入るものを a ～ e から選んでみましょう（1つ不要な選択肢があります）。

The roles of fathers in the animal kingdom
↓
(¹   )
↓
(²   )
↓
(³   )
↓
(⁴   )
↓
How a male emperor penguin feeds his chicks

a. A male bird raising his chicks without a nest

b. A male bird raising his children without the mother

c. An effective way for a male water bug to catch prey

d. How a hardhead catfish protects its eggs

e. The male water bug's hardship in raising children

▶️ Video-Viewing 2

以下は映像の内容をまとめたものです。
空所に適語を入れましょう。

Animal dads and their hard work

Species	Details of work
seahorse	The male gives birth to _____.
hardhead catfish	The male holds as many as _____ in his _____ and doesn't eat to avoid _____ any of the eggs. And he _____ for over two months while the eggs develop.
water bug	The females lay up to 100 eggs on the male's _____. He'll carry the eggs for _____ weeks.
rhea	The male _____ with about 5 to 7 females. The females lay their eggs in his nest and then quickly go away, _____ him to raise and defend all 30 or so chicks until they're about _____ old.
emperor penguin	Males keep the egg _____ atop their feet and away from the _____ _____. The dad manages to regurgitate some _____ from his esophagus to _____ the chick.

📖 Reading

次の文を読んで、あとの問いに答えましょう。　

For Fathers Everywhere

　To appreciate mothers, many countries celebrate Mother's Day. In the U.S., Anna Jarvis is credited with creating this day in 1908, which became an official holiday six years later. As to Father's Day, however, its birth took much longer and is attributed not to a man, but an American female, too.

5　Sonora Smart Dodd was one of six children raised by a single parent, her father. One day in 1909, while attending a church sermon to celebrate Mother's Day, she wondered why there was no equivalent celebration for fathers. Subsequently, she began to petition for such a holiday but received little support from society. Then, in the 1920s, to boost sales, the clothing industry became interested in the idea of
10　creating a day for fathers. A decade later, retailers decided to focus their efforts as much on a day to celebrate fathers as the already-recognized day to celebrate mothers.

Despite this raised awareness, and even the support of various presidents, it took decades for the idea to become widely accepted throughout the land. Eventually, though, in 1966, American President Lyndon Johnson made Father's Day a holiday— but not an official one—on the third Sunday of June. However, Dodd's dream was truly achieved when in 1972 President Richard Nixon declared it an official holiday.

Father's Day is celebrated on different days in different countries. Across Scandinavia, the American date was adopted in the 1930s, but in 1949 it was moved to the second Sunday in November. Part of the reason was to relocate it half a year away from Mother's Day. Perhaps it was also related to the Scandinavian concept of equality, which includes male participation in parenting.

In fact, year after year, countries such as Sweden, Norway, and Finland achieve the highest evaluations for their paternity leave systems, which allow fathers to stop working temporarily to share the task of looking after their newly born babies. Surprisingly, Japan is also one of the top countries in the world for its paternity leave system at 30 weeks. However, in terms of the percentage of fathers who actually take it, the figure is one of the lowest.

(355 words)

1. When did Mother's Day become an official holiday in the U.S?

    a. 1909

    b. 1914

    c. 1966

    d. 1972

2. Initially, who thought of the idea of Father's Day?

    a. Anna Jarvis

    b. Lyndon Johnson

    c. Richard Nixon

    d. Sonora Smart Dodd

3. Why did the clothing industry come to be interested in Father's Day?

_____

_____

4. What is a paternity leave system?

_____

_____

5. Why did Scandinavian countries relocate Father's Day in 1949? Give two reasons.

① _____

② _____

✍ Writing

あなたは emperor penguin の子供で、親鳥へ感謝のメールを送ります。感謝する点を3つ挙げて、親鳥へのメールを完成させましょう。

（感謝する点）

1. [　　　　　　　　] **2.** [　　　　　　　　] **3.** [　　　　　　　　]

Dear Dad,

I'm writing this e-mail to express my gratitude to you for you raising me and helping me grow this big. You've sacrificed a lot of things to take care of me. For example, often _____. You also _____. Also, it is amazing of you to _____ _____.

Thinking of all those things, I must say "How kind of you!"

Your son / daughter,

👉 Useful Expressions「感謝を伝える表現」

Thank you, indeed. / It's (That's) very kind of you. / How kind of you!

🔊 Speaking and Discussion   🎧 DL 07   ◎ CD 1-15   online audio

次の Daisuke と Emma の会話を聞いて内容を理解しましょう。その後ペアを組み、各自 Daisukei と Emma になって Useful Expressions を参考に、会話の続きをつくってみましょう。

Daisuke: My gosh! Finland 82%, Sweden 74%, Norway 72%, Japan 6%...

Emma: What are you talking about? What are those figures?

Daisuke: The percentages of fathers taking paternity leave in the world in 2013.

Emma: I see. You're disappointed about Japan's figure, aren't you?

Daisuke: Yeah, it's a real shame. The percentage is far too low.

Emma: I understand. Because even in my country, Norway, the ratio was less than 10% before the law encouraging fathers to take the leave was enforced in 1993.

· · · · · · · · · · · · · ↓続き↓ ·

Daisuke: Oh, really? But still, I had acutally hoped _____

_____ .

Emma: _____ .

Daisuke: _____ .

Emma: _____ .

👉 Useful Expressions

「失望、がっかりした気持ちを示す表現」

I'm disappointed about ... / ... is a great pity (disappointment).

I was hoping ... / That's too bad. / That's a shame. / I had actually hoped ...

UNIT 3
Life with Spice!

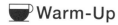Warm-Up

映像の写真をヒントに内容を予測して、次の質問に英語で答えましょう。

1. *How do you feel when you eat spicy food?*

....

....

2. *Why do people enjoy spicy food?*

....

....

these chemicals
phoria similar
's high"

▶️ Video-Viewing 1

(online video) (online audio)

🎧 DL 08   💿 CD 1-16

ビデオを見て、各キーワードを映像が出てくる順序に並べた場合、空所に入るものを
a ～ e から選んでみましょう（1つ不要な選択肢があります）。

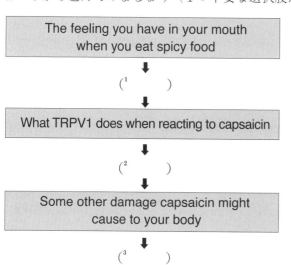

The feeling you have in your mouth
when you eat spicy food

↓

(¹   )

↓

What TRPV1 does when reacting to capsaicin

↓

(²   )

↓

Some other damage capsaicin might
cause to your body

↓

(³   )

↓

(⁴   )

a. Reasons why we enjoy spicy food

b. Various kinds of hot spices

c. A factor which determines your body's response to spicy food

d. A chemical compound in hot peppers

e. How your body reacts

 Video-Viewing 2

以下は映像の内容をまとめたものです。
空所に適語を入れましょう。

DL 08　CD 1-16

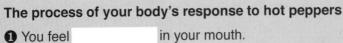

The process of your body's response to hot peppers

❶ You feel _____ in your mouth.

The chemical compound _____ is released, and it binds to

_____ _____ called TRPV1.

❷ TRPV1 sends warning signals to the brain.

❸ Your body tries to _____ itself _____ .

3 health risks spicy food might cause ——⟨ _____ in the throat

_____

└ anaphylactic _____

Reasons why people love spicy food

endrophins + dopamine = _____

 Reading

次の文を読んで、あとの問いに答えましょう。　DL 09　CD 1-17 ~ CD 1-21

online audio

No Scraps, Please

　Recently there has been much interest in the healthy properties of spices, with studies suggesting the benefits of consuming different types for different physical and mental ailments. But what we eat, our pets sometimes eat too, and this can have negative consequences.

5　If you have a pet dog, do you ever give it scraps of leftover food from your plate? If you do, think again—certain spices in human food could adversely affect the health of your beloved animal. For instance, garlic, a popular spice among humans, is thought to be dangerous for dogs. While not toxic to us, it is considered highly poisonous to them. Nutmeg is also toxic to canines and may cause them a severe

10　stomach upset, and agitate the nervous system, making a dog extremely excited then severely exhausted.

While humans love drinks made with cocoa powder, vets recommend that we never give this spice to dogs. The powder contains a compound similar to caffeine, which is harmful to the animal's nervous system and can contribute to kidney trouble and heart problems. Another human favorite is chocolate, but like cocoa, it is poisonous to canines, causing vomiting and even heart  seizures. Moreover, the darker the chocolate and the smaller the dog, the greater the danger is.

15

20

Yet, certain spices have benefits for canines. Take basil, for example. It helps reduce pain caused by arthritis, which is especially beneficial for older animals. 25 Moreover, it relieves stress and anxiety. People often remark that dogs have bad breath, but cinnamon (and parsley) can improve this problem, and the antioxidants it contains is effective in countering the effects of diabetes. To give a boost to a canine's digestive system and blood circulation, ginger root is said to have merits.

But one particular spice often touted as the king of healthy spices is turmeric. 30 Researchers have noted that it raises the metabolism, helps to accelerate weight loss, is effective against joint issues, and has benefits for a healthy brain and heart. So, if your pet dog eats your leftover curry every now and then, it may not be a bad thing at all.

(351 words)

1. What herb is useful for your pet dog when s/he has pain?

   a. garlic   **b.** basil

   c. nutmeg   **d.** cinnamon

2. Why do vets say it is not a good idea to let your pet dog drink cocoa?

   a. Because it helps reduce bad breath, but might cause decayed teeth.

   b. Because it enhances blood circulation so much that s/he becomes too excited.

   c. Because it usually has much more sugar that s/he needs per day.

   d. Because it contains a chemical compound that causes damage to his/her nerve system.

3. Which herb is said to be good for a dog that has a stomach problem?

_____

_____

4. Why is garlic considered to be bad for a dog?

_____

_____

5. How does turmeric work to improve our health?

_____

_____

🖋 Writing

イギリス人の Tom から、お勧めのスパイス料理の店を教えて、と頼まれました。店を紹介する前に、スパイシーな料理を 3 種類挙げて、Tom に好みを尋ねるメールを完成させましょう。

（スパイシー料理の種類）

1. [   ]   **2.** [   ]   **3.** [   ]

Dear Tom,

So you want to eat some spicy food in my town? Well, you have three choices, and they offer food from different parts of the world, so I'd like to know your preference. Which type of cuisine do you _____:

(1) _____ or (2) _____? Or do you prefer

(3) _____ food? Of course, you might want to know how much it

costs, but that depends on the time you go. _____ for

lunch or dinner? Let me know the details.

👉 **Useful Expressions 「好みを尋ねる表現」**

Which do you prefer, A or B? / Which do you like better, A or B? / Would you like to ...?
What would you prefer? / What would you like to ...? / What would you rather do?

🔊 Speaking and Discussion　 DL 10　 CD 1-22　(online / audio)

次の Bob と Aki の会話を聞いて内容を理解しましょう。その後ペアを組み、各自 Bob と Aki になって Useful Expressions を参考に、会話の続きをつくってみましょう。

Bob: Aki! Help me! My dog just ate a lot of chocolate and I don't know what to do. What should I do?

Aki: What? Your puppy ate chocolate? Oh, no. You should take her to a vet immediately.

Bob: A vet? OK. I'll call a taxi and go now. What else should I do?

Aki: You should calm down and be ready for the questions your vet may ask.

Bob: Like what?

· · · · · · · · · · · · · · · ↓続き↓ ·

Aki: First, you should tell _____

_____ .

Bob: OK, that's easy. It was about 10 minutes ago. What else?

Aki: _____

_____ .

Bob: _____ .

👉 Useful Expressions

「義務、強いお勧めを表す表現」

You should ... / You ought to ... / You must ... / It's better to ...

UNIT 4
The Importance of Insects

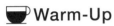 **Warm-Up**

映像の写真をヒントに内容を予測して、次の質問に英語で答えましょう。

1. *In what ways do insects help the environment on Earth?*

   ....

   ....

2. *If all the insects on Earth disappeared, what would happen?*

   ....

   ....

 **Video-Viewing 1**

 online video   online audio

 DL 11   CD 1-23

ビデオを見て、各キーワードを映像が出てくる順序に並べた場合、空所に入るものを a〜e から選んでみましょう（1つ不要な選択肢があります）。

```
┌─────────────────────────────┐
│   Daily life without insects │
└─────────────────────────────┘
              ↓
           (¹      )
              ↓
           (²      )
              ↓
┌─────────────────────────────┐
│ An example: Australian dung beetles │
└─────────────────────────────┘
              ↓
           (³      )
              ↓
┌─────────────────────────────────────┐
│ The serious problem we would face    │
│ without flesh-eating beetles and other insects │
└─────────────────────────────────────┘
              ↓
           (⁴      )
```

a. Possible outcomes of the world without dung beetles

b. The final situation of the world without insects

c. What would happen without cockroaches

d. What would happen without mosquitoes

e. Cicadas disturbing our life

▶️🎥 Video-Viewing 2

以下は映像の内容をまとめたものです。
空所に適語を入れましょう。

online / video   online / audio

🎧 DL 11   ⊙ CD 1-23

Positive aspect of some insects

Name	Number of species	Positive aspects
mosquitoes	over ____	They are food to birds, ____, ____, and other animals.
roaches	____	They are a ____ - ____ meal for birds, rodents, and even humans in some parts of the world.

What happened in Australia

- In ____, the ____ introduced cows to Australia.
- ____ cow poops enough to fill ____ tennis courts every year.
- The native Australian beetles wouldn't touch the poop because they evolved to eat only ____, ____ marsupial dung.
- By ____ the cattle had carpeted ____ acres of pasture in dung. But too much ____ makes it impossible for anything to grow.

What would happen to us in a world without any insects?

⋯⋯▶ We would ____ to death or drown in a sea of ____ and ____.

📖 Reading

次の文を読んで、あとの問いに答えましょう。   🎧 DL 12   ⊙ CD 1-24 ~ ⊙ CD 1-29

online / audio

The Greatest Survivors

Evolution on Earth has produced many winners and losers, as certain species of animal and plant life have continued to develop and transform while others have experienced little change or even become extinct. Regarding the more successful ones, humans may hold a common consensus that we are the masters of survival,
5 since we dominate the planet. Or do we?

Wherever you go on Earth, you will not always find people. However, you will always come across insects. They are true experts of survival, having existed for nearly half a billion years and avoiding mass extinction events that have wiped out other animal groups, most notably dinosaurs. Clearly, their success is due to an
10 ability to adapt quickly to diverse environments and new opportunities.

In order to gain a deeper understanding about the evolutionary path of these masters of survival and adaptation, scientists recently undertook a major research project. Using DNA sequence data of an unprecedented scale and new analysis techniques, they were able to look further back in time than previous studies and analyze the evolutionary path of insects from as far back as 500 million years ago.

At that time, insects were evolving from water-based crustaceans, such as crabs, lobsters and prawns, to land-dwelling creatures. These first land insects were wingless, but around 400 million years ago they began to develop them, enabling quicker, easier and unrestricted mobility from region to region. Yet, this was not the only major change occurring at the time—there was also the emergence of the earliest terrestrial plants. As such, this was a coincidence that proved to have a major impact on how the earliest ecosystems were shaped.

Yet, the majority of major insect groups that people are familiar with today emerged in two period bursts. For example, cockroaches and grasshoppers, appeared around 350 million years ago. Subsequently, numerous common insects, such as flies, wasps and beetles, materialized around 150 million years later.

So, considering their amazing journey of evolution, the next time you see one of these small creatures, instead of treating it with contempt and possibly trying to eliminate it, appreciate its mastery of survival. (354 words)

1. According to the reading passage, what are the masters of survival?

   a. crustaceans

   b. dinosaurs

   c. insects

   d. people

2. Around 400 million years ago, what ability did insects acquire?

   a. the ability to breathe underwater water

   b. the ability to communicate with each other through sound

   c. the ability to dwell on land

   d. the ability to fly from one place to another

3. What made it possible for insects to survive for over half a billion years in nature?

_____

_____

4. What insects emerged 200 million years ago?

_____

_____

5. How did insects evolve 500 million years ago?

_____

_____

✍ Writing

日本の山へ初めてキャンプに行くモンゴル人の Zaya に、害虫対策として取るべき方法を教えてあげました。あなたが考えた害虫対策を3つ挙げて、それを確認する Zaya へのメールを完成させましょう。

（害虫対策）

1. [   ]   **2.** [   ]   **3.** [   ]

Hello Zaya,

I'm sure you're excited about your first camping experience in Japan. I do hope you enjoy it, and I'd like to remind you what to do about annoying insects. First, _____ since your camping site is far from any convenience stores. Also, did you remember _____? I expect you've already _____, but _____ _____. If you take these measures, you don't have to worry too much. You can just enjoy yourself!

☞ Useful Expressions「再確認するための表現」

Did you remember to …? / Don't forget… / Can [Could] I remind you…? / I'd like to remind you…
Will you remember to …? / I expect you've already done it, but…

📢 Speaking and Discussion 🎧 DL 13 ◉ CD 1-30 (online / audio)

次の Carol と Daisuke の会話を聞いて内容を理解しましょう。その後ペアを組み、各自 Carol と Daisuke になって Useful Expressions を参考に、会話の続きをつくってみましょう。

Daisuke: Wow, these people in South America say they get protein from insects!

Carol: It's not that surprising. People also eat insects in some parts of Japan.

Daisuke: Really?

Carol: Yes. Actually, I was offered locusts in Nagano.

Daisuke: Locusts!!

Carol: Don't be surprised. I tried them, and they weren't bad. Actually, I think eating insects is getting more and more popular among those who are interested in SDGs.

· ↓続き↓ ·

Daisuke: _____.

Carol: At first, I found it very surprising, but eating less meat is good for your health, too._____.

Daisuke: _____.

Carol: _____.

👉 Useful Expressions

「信じられないという感情を表す表現」

Really? / I don't believe it! / What a surprise! / That's a surprise.
That's amazing. / That's surprising. / Are you serious?
You must be joking. / You're kidding. / I find that very surprising.

UNIT 5
Suits for Discovery

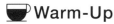 Warm-Up

映像の写真をヒントに内容を予測して、次の質問に英語で答えましょう。

1.
What are some potential problems of space travel?

....

....

2.
What is the advantage of the white spacesuits the astronauts are wearing?

....

....

▶️ Video-Viewing 1

online video　online audio　🎧 DL 14　◎ CD 1-31

ビデオを見て、各キーワードを映像が出てくる順序に並べた場合、空所に入るものを a ～ e から選んでみましょう（1つ不要な選択肢があります）。

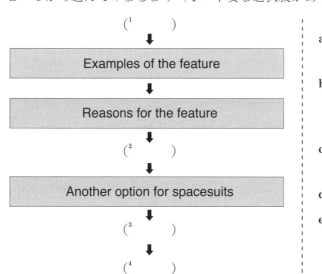

(¹　　)
↓

Examples of the feature
↓

Reasons for the feature
↓

(²　　)
↓

Another option for spacesuits
↓

(³　　)
↓

(⁴　　)

a. Dangers astronauts face in space

b. Concerns about future space exploration and possible solutions

c. How the first astronauts landed on the moon

d. A common feature of spacesuits

e. The next destination in space travel

 Video-Viewing 2

以下は映像の内容をまとめたものです。
空所に適語を入れましょう。

DL 14   CD 1-31

Risks astronauts face caused by
- blistering _____.
- severe _____.
- _____ damage.

The color variation of spacesuits and gadgets used by astronauts

Color	When?	Why?
white	currently	White reflects _____'s _____ effectively.
_____ orange	currently / heading into space or coming home	Orange _____ in the ocean and the sky.
_____ blue	starting to use it	In the case of an emergency, rescue teams can rely on more _____ ways of locating crews such as _____ _____ and _____.

📖 Reading

次の文を読んで、あとの問いに答えましょう。   DL 15   CD 1-32 ~ CD 1-35

online audio

The Problem of Making Spacesuits

It is no coincidence that the average person's image of an astronaut is male rather than female. After all, most people know that the first human to walk on the surface of the Moon was the famous Apollo 11 astronaut Neil Armstrong, followed by his crewmate, Buzz Aldrin on July 20, 1969. As males, they represented the
5 typical image of humans, exploring space for the benefit of mankind.

On land, women also played vital roles in space exploration. For example, seamstresses made the spacesuits of the Apollo 11 crew, which consisted of 21 layers of synthetics, neoprene rubber, and metalized polyester. Such a multitude of layers was necessary to protect the astronauts from the Moon's severe
10 temperatures, from over 100 degrees to -150 degrees Celsius in the shade. The skilled women hand-crafted the spacesuits with extreme care and precision since

one stitching error greater than 0.79 mm meant that a spacesuit could have been rejected as unsafe.

15

In space, the presence of female astronauts has brought about changes to the design of spacesuits. Every early NASA spacesuit was designed for the male torso. But these tailor-made suits were costly, so the organization decided to use reusable suits that had changeable arm, leg and torso components. Then, with women being accepted into NASA's astronaut training program from the late 70s, it created the problem of fit due to differences in dimension between the male and female body. However, trial and error led to the creation of components for building the right suit for the right body regardless of gender.

20

25

NASA now has a goal of putting a man and woman on the Moon in 2024. Yet, for this task, they decided to return to the early method of individually-fitting spacesuits, though they will be more sophisticated. The mission's selected astronauts will have a full-body 3-D scan in various postures. The purpose is to ensure that each astronaut's spacesuit is a perfect fit, providing maximum comfort and the broadest range of physical motion. When they do step onto the Moon, headlines around the world may read: "One small step for women, one giant leap for humankind."

30

(354 words)

1. Why do people typically have the image of astronauts as being male?
   a. Because males symbolize human exploration and landed on the Moon first.
   b. Because male astronauts have more physical strength than female ones.
   c. Because all early NASA spacesuits were made to fit the male body.
   d. Because females have made little contribution to space exploration.

2. What was the distinctive characteristic of spacesuits for the crew of Apollo 11?
   a. They had multi-layers.
   b. They were machine-made.
   c. They had changeable components.
   d. They fitted perfectly.

3. Why did the spacesuits for Apollo 11 have to be carefully made?

_____

_____

4. What problem did NASA start having upon accepting female astronauts?

_____

_____

5. What will NASA do to the crew going to the Moon in 2024, and why will they do it?

_____

_____

✍ Writing

ベトナムのメル友の Anh（アイン）から「宇宙飛行士になりたい」と相談を受けました。「国際宇宙ステーション搭乗飛行士募集要項」等を参考にして、宇宙飛行士に必要な資格等を３項目上げてみましょう。その後、下の文章の空欄を埋めて、彼女へのメールを完成させましょう。

（宇宙飛行士に求める条件）

1. ┌────────────┐ 2. ┌────────────┐ 3. ┌────────────┐

Dear Anh,

I actually found some information about the requirements for an astronaut on the Internet. First, _____ .You also _____ _____ . According to the site I checked, you are required to _____ , too. Proficiency in English is a must when you want to be a crew at the International Space Station, but you don't have to worry about it at all since you are already very fluent!

📌 Useful Expressions「必要性を表す表現」
You should ... / You need to ... / You are required to ... / You must ... / You ought to ... /
You are supposed to ... / You are expected to... / ... is needed / ... is a must

📢 Speaking and Discussion  DL 16 ⦿ CD 1-36  online audio

次の Becky と Akira の会話を聞いて内容を理解しましょう。その後ペアを組み、各自 Becky と Akira になって Useful Expressions を参考に、会話の続きをつくってみましょう。

Becky: Look at this advertisement. Space travel is starting! You can buy a seat on a spaceship if you want.

Akira: Well, I don't know if that can be a destination for a future trip.

Becky: Why not?

Akira: Because, first of all, the price for a seat must be rocket-high!

Becky: Yes, but you might win a lottery someday!

· · · · · · · · · · · · · ↓続き↓ ·

Akira: That's impossible! The possibility of winning a lottery is less than that of being hit by a car.

Becky: Yeah, but anyway, you ought to have a dream in life. _____
_____ .

Akira: _____
_____ .

Becky: _____
_____ .

👉 Useful Expressions

「可能性を表す表現」
That's (quite / very / perfectly) possible. / It's (quite / very) likely.
It may ... / It might ... / It could …
Maybe ... / Perhaps ….

「可能性がないことを示す表現」
That's not possible. / That's (quite) impossible. / It's not likely. / It's unlikely.
That'll never happen.

UNIT 6
Changing Bodies

 **Warm-Up**

映像の写真をヒントに内容を予測して、次の質問に英語で答えましょう。

1. *What changes have happened to the human body in the past 130 years?*

....

....

2. *What changes will happen to our human body if humans could live on Mars?*

....

....

 Video-Viewing 1

online / video   online / audio

DL 17   CD 1-37

ビデオを見て、各キーワードを映像が出てくる順序に並べた場合、空所に入るものを a〜e から選んでみましょう（1つ不要な選択肢があります）。

```
The average height of humans
1,000 years from now
        ↓
      ( ¹      )
        ↓
Some changes inside our body
      ( ²      )
        ↓
      ( ³      )
        ↓
      ( ⁴      )
        ↓
The faster we change,
the better our chance of surviving.
```

a. A new experiment: transplanting heads

b. Our shorter ancestors

c. Manipulating genes with gene-editing tools

d. New physical abilities that humans might acquire

e. Possible changes people might experience on Mars

 Video-Viewing 2

online / video　online / audio

以下は映像の内容をまとめたものです。
空所に適語を入れましょう。

DL 17　CD 1-37

Possible changes inside and outside of our bodies in 1,000 years

- We will be _____ .
- With hearing aids, we can _____ sounds, generate _____ _____ , and the aids will come with a _____ phone.
- With _____ eyes, we will see what we currently consider invisible, such as _____ and _____ .
- With _____ tools like CRISPR, we may control our genes and DNA to make ourselves _____ to disease.

Possible changes on Mars ┬ 33% less sunlight ➡ _____ pupils
　　　　　　　　　　　　　└ 62% less gravity ➡ _____ _____ anyone on Earth

The path to immortality is ┬ to download human _____ into machines.
　　　　　　　　　　　　　　 └ to _____ human heads.

 Reading

次の文を読んで、あとの問いに答えましょう。　DL 18　CD 1-38 ~ CD 1-42

online / audio

Freezing for the Future

　How long do you want to live? For most people, the answer is probably "longer," but often, it is decided by serious health issues. Accordingly, there is constant effort by private and public organizations to improve human health and explore ways of extending our lives.

　According to the World Health Organization, between 2000 and 2016, global
5　average life expectancy experienced a significant rise of 5.5 years, averaging 72 years for men and women. While this is good news, for many scientists and researchers, an initial goal may be a hundred years. But regardless of the figure, the human body has physical limitations that presently appear impossible to overcome. Inevitably, aging leads to a natural reduction of performance in the
10　biological functions of the human body to a point where it can no longer support itself.

Despite this obstacle, science marches on in search of solutions, and one has appeared in the form of cryopreservation. This is a process that involves freezing body organs and tissue at very low temperatures in order to preserve, and then revive them in the future to enable others to live. Yet, one of the main problems of this process has not been the freezing but the thawing. When specimens thaw out, ice crystals form and these can damage the tissue, which in turn can render the organs unusable.

While many scientists doubt the future success of cryogenic techniques, progress has been made by believers of the process. Namely, frozen specimens have been successfully rewarmed without causing damage to the all-important tissue. The key was in preventing the formation of damaging ice crystals by using nanoparticles to heat tissue at an equal rate.

This work has great importance for people awaiting organ transplants. Contrary to common belief, there is usually not a lack of organ donors. Currently, the problem is that organs can only be preserved for a few hours, but it often takes longer to find suitable recipients and transport the organs in time. Hopefully, with further success in cryopreservation, the whole process can be perfected to protect the lives of those in urgent need of a transplant.

(353 words)

1. How old was the average life expectancy just prior to 2000?
   a. About 66.5 years
   b. About 72 years
   c. More than 72 years
   d. Less than 66 years

2. What should be overcome if people want to live longer than 100 years?
   a. The effort by researchers to march on in organ-transplanting experiments
   b. A natural reduction in the biological functions of the human body
   c. Physical limitations that stop scientists from performing longevity research
   d. Human health that extends our lives longer and longer

3. What is cryopreservation?

_____

_____

4. What is the biggest problem in cryopreservation, and why does it occur?

_____

_____

5. For whom is cryopreservation most beneficial now?

_____

_____

✍ Writing

中国人研究者 Dr. Bing Su が「ヒトの脳を発達させる遺伝子をサルへ移植して成功した」といういうニュース記事を読みました。この研究について知りたいことを3つ挙げて、Dr. Suへのメールを完成させましょう。

（研究について知りたいこと）

1.	2.	3.

Dear Dr. Bing Su,

I am a Japanese university student, and my name is _____.
I read a newspaper article saying you've succeeded in putting human brain
genes into monkeys. So, I'd like to know more about your research. First, _____
_____? I also would like to know _____
_____. Lastly, _____
_____? I would be happy if I could read your scientific
article answering these questions in detail someday, especially if it were easy
enough for non-professionals (like me) to understand.

☞ Useful Expressions「色々な質問をするための表現」

Where (When, Why, How) did you...?
Where (When, Why, How) was the experiment(research) ...? / I'd like to know ...

🔊 Speaking and Discussion　🎧 DL 19　◉ CD 1-43　(online/audio)

次の Akira と Becky の会話を聞いて内容を理解しましょう。その後ペアを組み、各自 Akira と Becky になって Useful Expressions を参考に、会話の続きをつくってみましょう。

Akira: Wow, this Japanese scientist is conducting research where he let AI technology learn human cognition so that a person's mind lives forever in the AI.

Becky: Do you really want to live forever after your body dies? I'm not that interested in immortality.

Akira: Really? Living so many years sounds very cool to me.

· ↓続き↓ ·

Becky: No, _____

_____ .

Akira: Yeah, humans are destined to die when the time comes. But still, I want to live as many years as I can.

Becky: _____ . I mean, you'll lose all your friends, and you'll be alone, just having clear memories of your good old days, right?

Akira: _____ .

👉 Useful Expressions

「反対を表す表現」
Not really. / No, I don't think so. / I disagree. / That's not the way I see…
I can't agree with that … / But isn't … more …? / Do you really think…?

32

UNIT 7
A Cold Thought

Warm-Up

映像の写真をヒントに内容を予測して、次の質問に英語で答えましょう。

1.

What would happen to New York if all the ice on Earth melted?

....

....

2.

What would happen underground if all the ice on Earth melted?

....

....

▶️🎥 Video-Viewing 1

ビデオを見て、各キーワードを映像が出てくる順序に並べた場合、空所に入るものを a～e から選んでみましょう（1つ不要な選択肢があります）。

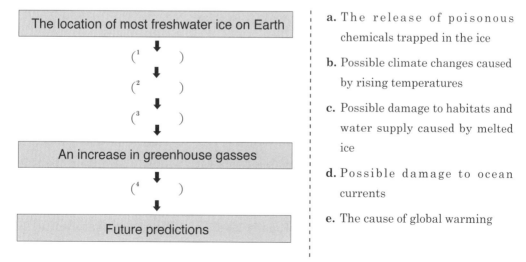

| The location of most freshwater ice on Earth |
| ⬇️ |
| (¹　　　) |
| ⬇️ |
| (²　　　) |
| ⬇️ |
| (³　　　) |
| ⬇️ |
| An increase in greenhouse gasses |
| ⬇️ |
| (⁴　　) |
| ⬇️ |
| Future predictions |

a. The release of poisonous chemicals trapped in the ice

b. Possible climate changes caused by rising temperatures

c. Possible damage to habitats and water supply caused by melted ice

d. Possible damage to ocean currents

e. The cause of global warming

 Video-Viewing 2

以下は映像の内容をまとめたものです。
空所に適語を入れましょう。

 DL 20 CD 1-44

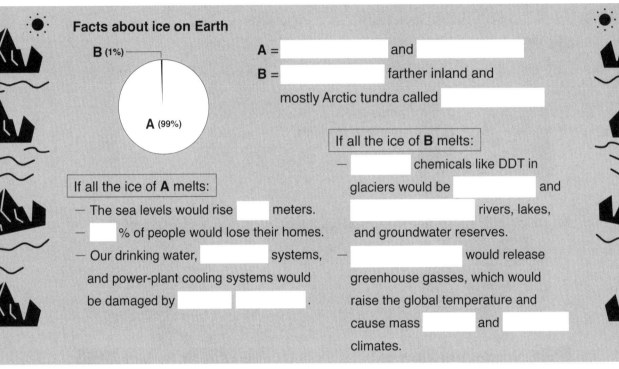

Facts about ice on Earth

B (1%)

A (99%)

A = [   ] and [   ]

B = [   ] farther inland and
mostly Arctic tundra called [   ]

If all the ice of A melts:
— The sea levels would rise [   ] meters.
— [   ] % of people would lose their homes.
— Our drinking water, [   ] systems,
  and power-plant cooling systems would
  be damaged by [   ] [   ].

If all the ice of B melts:
— [   ] chemicals like DDT in
  glaciers would be [   ] and
  [   ] rivers, lakes,
  and groundwater reserves.
— [   ] would release
  greenhouse gasses, which would
  raise the global temperature and
  cause mass [   ] and [   ]
  climates.

 Reading

次の文を読んで、あとの問いに答えましょう。 DL 21 CD 1-45 ~ CD 1-48

Is "Ice" Just "Ice"?

When people think of the word "ice," the first image that may spring to mind is the mechanically-made ice cubes in our fridges at home. But in the natural world, ice is, of course, created naturally on far larger scales. Moreover, this type exists in a variety of formations, with each one telling the story of its surrounding

5 environment and providing a historical record of climate change in that particular region. As such, the formations provide scientists with valuable data from the past as well as potential hints for predicting future climatic patterns on Earth.

One type of large freshwater ice formation found on every continent is the glacier. This kind of formation is the result of many layers of falling snow that eventually

10 become so heavy that they are compressed into ice. From a distance, glaciers appear to be rivers of ice that have come to an abrupt halt. Yet, they are constantly

moving downward inch by inch, year by year, and can extend for several hundred miles. However, with the rise in global temperatures, some are clearly shrinking in size.

While glaciers appear on land, perhaps the most well-known type of ice formation—but found in the oceans—is the iceberg. For many people, this type may make them automatically recall the movie *The Titanic*, where the maiden voyage of the ship by that name was tragically ended by an unseen iceberg in the Atlantic Ocean in April 1912. While nine-tenths of an iceberg is underwater, to be classified as one requires the visible part to be 4.9 meters above the surface, be 30 to 50 meters thick and cover a minimum area of 500 square meters.

Back on land, the largest, yet less well-known ice formations in the world are ice sheets. These massive entities can cover over 50,000 square kilometers, and may be the most important ones for the human race. During the last Ice Age, such sheets covered large parts of North and South America as well as northern Europe but have long since vanished. Today, only three remain, covering Greenland, West Antarctica and East Antarctica. Can you guess when these ones might disappear, too?

(360 words)

1. What do people typically imagine when they hear the word "ice"?

   a. icebergs in the ocean

   b. ice sheets on land

   c. glaciers in the mountains

   d. ice cubes in the fridge

2. What requirements must be met for an ice block in the ocean to be classified as an iceberg?

   a. Its area, height, and thickness

   b. Its thickness and the coverage of the sea

   c. The ratio of its visible part and underwater part

   d. The speed of floating and its area

3. What ice formations can we see in the world?

_____

_____

4. How is a glacier formed?

_____

_____

5. Why are ice formations in the world considered to be important?

_____

_____

✍ Writing

エジプト人の友人 Eva から川の近くに住むことになったので災害への備えを教えて欲しい、と頼まれました。河川災害への対策として考えられるものを 3 つ挙げて、Eva へのメールを完成させましょう。

（河川災害への対策）

1. [　　　　　　　] **2.** [　　　　　　　] **3.** [　　　　　　　]

Dear Eva,

How's life in your new a house just beside a river? I would advise you to take

every measure to protect yourself in case of emergency. First, _____

_____, which will help you a lot if you have to

evacuate. Be careful _____.

Also, make sure you _____ _____

_____. You can't be too careful when there is the possibility

of any disaster from happening.

👉 **Useful Expressions 「～に注意して、という表現」**

Be careful not to … / Be ready for … / Make sure you don't … / Make sure you do…

🔊 Speaking and Discussion　🎧 DL 22　💿 CD 1-49　(online audio)

次の Becky と Akira の会話を聞いて内容を理解しましょう。その後ペアを組み、各自
Becky と Akira になって Useful Expressions を参考に、会話の続きをつくってみましょ
う。

Becky: Look at this article! It says if you live close to the sea, you might face the danger of losing your home.

Akira: Yeah, I know. If the sea level rises because of global warming, it might happen. But still, I like living along the seacoast much more than living in the countryside.

Becky: Really? For me, rural inland areas are better than the seaside. You can enjoy more greenery.

Akira: You're right, but if you compare the two areas, you'll find it's much more attractive to live near the sea. There are just so many better reasons.

Becky: Like what?

· ↓続き↓ ·

Akira: _____

_____.

Becky: Is that so? _____.

Akira: _____.

Becky: _____.

👉 Useful Expressions

「比較を表す表現」

If you compare A and B, ... / Compared to ... / I like A better than B

... is (greatly) superior / ... is (greatly) superior (inferior)

... is better (worse) than / ... is 比較級 (–er / more ...) than

You just can't compare ...

UNIT 8
No Space for Wisdom

Warm-Up

映像の写真をヒントに内容を予測して、次の質問に英語で答えましょう。

1.  *How did ancient people use their wisdom teeth?*

   ....

   ....

2.  *What happens in your mouth when there is not enough space for teeth?*

   ....

   ....

▶◼ Video-Viewing 1

DL 23   CD 2-02

ビデオを見て、各キーワードを映像が出てくる順序に並べた場合、空所に入るものを a～e から選んでみましょう（1つ不要な選択肢があります）。

The number of people who suffer from wisdom teeth problems and the cost
↓
(¹　　　)
↓
(²　　　)
↓
No space for wisdom teeth
↓
(³　　　)
↓
(⁴　　　)
↓
The risks of surgery for removing wisdom teeth

a. The evolution of our body and teeth

b. Problems wisdom teeth may cause

c. Dentists' treatment to save other teeth

d. How seriously wisdom teeth could get damaged

e. The way our ancestors used wisdom teeth

▶️ Video-Viewing 2

以下は映像の内容をまとめたものです。
空所に適語を入れましょう。

online video   online audio

🎧 DL 23   ◎ CD 2-02

Facts about Teeth

■ _____ people get their wisdom teeth removed in the U.S. every year.

■ Apart from wisdom teeth, people have _____ molars.

■ Wisdom teeth usually grow between the _____ of _____ and _____ .

■ _____ was the trigger of wisdom teeth problems.

■ The _____ that determine the size of our jaws are completely separate
from the _____ that determine how many teeth we grow.

Wisdom Teeth Problems

— grow in at odd _____ , press against _____ , causing swelling and pain.

— form narrow crevices and create _____ _____ .

— attract _____ and cause infection and _____ _____ .

📖 Reading

次の文を読んで、あとの問いに答えましょう。   🎧 DL 24   ◎ CD 2-03 ～ ◎ CD 2-06

online audio

Smile, Please!

In modern society, having a nice set of teeth is usually seen as an advantage
in life. Long, long ago, however, teeth were simply tools for survival, and our
ancestors probably cared little about their appearance. Naturally, thousands of
years ago there were no toothbrushes, toothpaste, mouthwash or dental floss
5 to keep them white and bright. Neither were there dentists with sophisticated
technology to treat them. This suggests that our ancestors experienced high levels
of tooth decay.

But scientific studies on early human fossils reveal our ancestors had relatively
good oral health. In fact, in pre-agricultural societies, instances of bad teeth
10 were very rare. For example, the frequency among hunter-gatherer societies was
approximately 1 to 5%. The problem of bad teeth actually appeared quite recently
in the history of the human race. Around 10,000 years ago, at the beginning of

the Neolithic period, our ancestors began cultivating land for farming. For these agriculturalists, the rates of tooth decay leapt and were anywhere between 10 and 80%. Clearly, this was due to a change in diet, which continues to this day. Globally, around 75% of children and nearly 100% of adults now have tooth decay.

But in today's society, apart from enabling us to eat, there are other reasons to avoid bad teeth. According to a recent study in the U.S., entitled *Behind the Smile*, when looking at images, around two-thirds of Americans said they were more likely to recall someone if they had a nice smile, and straight white teeth are central to this facial expression. Additionally, straight teeth were seen as a sign of happiness (21%), smartness (38%), and good health (47%). The study also found that Americans perceive people with straight teeth as 58% more likely to be successful and wealthy. Moreover, around three-quarters answered that they are more likely to trust someone who has a nice smile.

Considering these statistics, and the fact that society is placing more and more emphasis on how people look, evidently there is great wisdom in looking after your teeth. Remember this when taking your next selfie!

(345 words)

1. How did the rates of teeth decay change after our ancestors started farming the land?

   a. They decreased by 1 to 5%.

   b. They increased between 10 and 80%.

   c. They decreased drastically.

   d. They increased about 10 times or more.

2. How do 75% of Americans think of a person with a nice smile?

   a. Trustworthy

   b. Outgoing

   c. Successful

   d. Wealthy

3. What did scientific studies on early human fossils find out about our ancestors?

_____

_____

4. According to the study *Behind the Smile*, what do Americans think straight teeth represent?

_____

_____

5. Why does the author think looking after our teeth is important?

_____

_____

✍ Writing

アメリカ人の友人 Cathy が、日本で歯科医院を探しています。あなたが歯科医に求める事柄を3項目挙げてみましょう。それから、Cathy に歯科医院を紹介するメールを完成させましょう。

（歯科医に求める条件）

1. [＿＿＿＿＿＿]   **2.** [＿＿＿＿＿＿]   **3.** [＿＿＿＿＿＿]

Dear Cathy,

  I heard you are looking for _____, and I can give you

some advice. In Japan, when you go to _____, you should

_____. Also, you ought to _____

_____. And don't forget to _____.

I hope this will help you. Call me anytime if you want to know more.

👉 Useful Expressions「提案する、アドバイスを与える」

Why don't you ...? / You should ... / You shouldn't ... / I advise you (not) to ...
Don't ... / Never ... / If I were you, I'd ... / Remember to ... / Don't forget to ...

🔊 Speaking and Discussion 🎧 DL 25 💿 CD 2-07 online audio

次の Aki と Bob の会話を聞いて内容を理解しましょう。その後ペアを組み、各自 Aki
と Bob になって Useful Expressions を参考に、会話の続きをつくってみましょう。

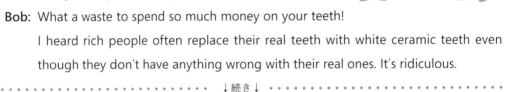

Aki: Wow, this actor has beautiful teeth! They're all straight
and white, and his smile is so charming.

Bob: Yeah, he has a really nice smile, but he should because
he's a professional actor. I think he always spends a lot
of money on maintaining his appearance, including
his teeth.

Aki: But it is nice to have shiny bright teeth. I would spend
all my money if I could get teeth like his.

Bob: What a waste to spend so much money on your teeth!
I heard rich people often replace their real teeth with white ceramic teeth even
though they don't have anything wrong with their real ones. It's ridiculous.

· ↓続き↓ ·

Aki: No, I don't think so because _____

_____.

Bob: Sorry, I don't agree with you. _____.

Aki: _____.

Bob: _____.

👉 Useful Expressions

「意見を述べる」
I believe / think / believe … / It seems to me that ….

「賛成する」
I think so, too. / I agree with you. / I think you're right. / That's very true.

「部分的に賛成する」
I see what you mean, but … / I agree with you in a sense, but … / But on the other hand, …
That may be true, but …

「反対する」
No, I don't think so. / Sorry, I don't agree (disagree) with you.

UNIT 9
Sounds from Plastic

 Warm-Up

映像の写真をヒントに内容を予測して、次の質問に英語で答えましょう。

1.
What do you think the speaker in the left picture is made from?

....

....

2.
Why was this speaker made?

....

....

▶◀ Video-Viewing 1

🎧 DL 26   ◉ CD 2-08

ビデオを見て、各キーワードを映像が出てくる順序に並べた場合、空所に入るものを a ～ e から選んでみましょう（1つ不要な選択肢があります）。

A start-up company producing
a unique product

↓

(¹   )

↓

(²   )

↓

The secret of each speaker's colors

↓

(³   )

↓

(⁴   )

a. This year's aim and the hope for the future

b. The company's ultimate goal

c. Introduction of the team members

d. The process of making a speaker

e. The reality of plastic waste

Video-Viewing 2

以下は映像の内容をまとめたものです。　　　　🎧 DL 26　　◎ CD 2-08
空所に適語を入れましょう。

A Start-up Company Called Gomi Designs

= "Gomi" means [   ], or [   ], in Japanese.

The Process of Making a Gomi Speaker

The designer and his team place [   ] plastic bags in the oven to [   ] them down. ➡ The melted sheets are mixed together and kneaded. ➡ They heat compression molds and fill them with [   ]. ➡ They place the molds into a [   ], then the speaker's components are [   ] -finished. ➡ The speaker's electrical components are [   ].

Three Reasons Why Plastic Is Not Recycled

1. It is [   ] to recycle.　　**2.** [   ] don't accept it.

3. Individuals don't put it into [   ].

Gomi Design's goal

To create [   ] products = products that can always be used again after being [   ].

Reading

次の文を読んで、あとの問いに答えましょう。　　🎧 DL 27　　◎ CD 2-09 ～ ◎ CD 2-13

Driving on Trash

The human race is very good at creating new things. Unfortunately, though, we excel at creating garbage and trash, too. While most of this unwanted material is put into landfills, a growing percentage is being recycled. Even so, we are constantly searching for even better ways of waste disposal using methods that
5　harm neither the environment nor its variety of inhabitants.

One positive change in the battle to help protect our planet's environment is the development of cars that no longer run on gasoline-polluting engines. But how would you feel about driving one along a road with thousands of plastic bags, bottles and toner from empty printer cartridges under your wheels? Perhaps you
10　imagine that your environmentally-friendly vehicle would soon come to a halt due to problems caused by the waste, such as your tires being punctured by pieces of

sharp glass. However, you would be wrong.

Just outside the Australian city of Melbourne there is a unique type of road that is paved with large amounts of recycled waste and asphalt, known as Reconophalt. In fact, if you drove along this road, under your wheels there would be a mountain of garbage equivalent to 200,000 plastic bags, 63,000 glass bottles and waste toner from 4,500 printer cartridges.

15

20

Yet, this is not the only such road in Australia, as hundreds of miles have actually been laid around the country. Moreover, interest in this waste-management system is growing in other nations, including the United States and the United Kingdom, who are both conducting trials. Such testing is necessary since different climates 25 can affect road performance, causing surfaces to crack or warp, especially in hot and humid ones.

Such weather-induced effects may lead to questions about the safety of roads built with large proportions of recycled material, and plastic in particular. However, laboratory tests have shown that even if global warming increased by 30 up to six degrees Celsius, there would be no change in the performance of roads constructed with Reconophalt. Clearly, all societies can appreciate the advantage of this method of hiding our waste. However, we must remember that our priority is to reduce it in the first place.

(358 words)

1. Where have Reconophalt roads already been tested?
   a. Australia
   b. the U.S.
   c. the U.K.
   d. All of the above

2. What is a typical but not environmentally-friendly way to deal with garbage?
   a. drive vehicles with non-gasoline engines
   b. put it into landfills
   c. recycle it for new materials
   d. reduce the garbage we create

3. Why are the trials on Reconophalt roads needed?

_____

_____

4. What have laboratory tests on Reconophalt roads shown?

_____

_____

5. What is the most crucial thing in waste management in society?

_____

_____

Writing

あなたは映像で紹介された Gomi Designs に興味をもち、海外インターンシップを申し込もうとしています。自分のセールスポイントを３つ挙げて、会社宛てのメールを完成させましょう。
（自分のセールスポイント）

1. [   ] **2.** [   ] **3.** [   ]

To Whom It May Concern,

Hello, I'm a Japanese student who is interested in your company. I'm wondering if you could accept me as an intern next summer. Let me tell you about myself.

First of all, I can _____ and _____

_____. Regarding your company, I'd say I'll be able

to _____. Above all, I'm interested

in creating a sustainable society, so I would like to learn more about your

activities while working for you.

👉 Useful Expressions「特技、得意なことを示す表現」

I have experience of ... / I believe I'll able to ... / I believe I have the ability to ...
I'm sure (certain / convinced) that I can ...

Speaking and Discussion DL 28  CD 2-14 online audio

次の Fumika と George の会話を聞いて内容を理解しましょう。その後ペアを組み、各自 Fumika と George になって Useful Expressions を参考に、会話の続きをつくってみましょう。

Fumika: Look! These speakers are made from old plastic bags. Isn't it amazing?

George: Yeah, it's incredible. But would you want to use something made from trash?

Fumika: Yes, I wouldn't mind. I think everyone should take action to create a sustainable society, and using recycled products is the first step. Otherwise, we may have no future at all.

· ↓続き↓ ·

George: Hm, I guess you're right. But I don't feel comfortable using something from a

trash can.

Fumika: Well, _____.

George: But still, personally, _____

_____.

Fumika: _____.

👉 Useful Expressions

「意見を述べる際の表現」

In my opinion (view) ... / Personally, I think (feel, believe) ...
From my point of view, ... / I'd also like to say (add) that ...

UNIT 10
Forward vs. Backward

☕Warm-Up

映像の写真をヒントに内容を予測して、次の質問に英語で答えましょう。

1.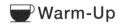
Which direction do trade winds usually blow?

....

....

2.
Travelling westbound or eastbound, which flight would get much shorter if if the Earth rotated backward?

....

▶◢ Video-Viewing 1

DL 29   CD 2-15

ビデオを見て、各キーワードを映像が出てくる順序に並べた場合、空所に入るものを a 〜 e から選んでみましょう（1つ不要な選択肢があります）。

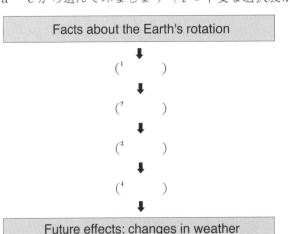

Facts about the Earth's rotation

↓
(¹   )
↓
(²   )
↓
(³   )
↓
(⁴   )
↓

Future effects: changes in weather and landscapes in North America

a. Future effects: changes in weather patterns in Europe

b. Future effects: shrinking deserts but increased plant life

c. Immediate changes caused by reverse prevailing westerlies

d. Immediate changes caused by reverse trade winds

e. What would happen while the Earth is slowing down to reverse direction

 Video-Viewing 2

以下は映像の内容をまとめたものです。
空所に適語を入れましょう。

 online video online audio

DL 29 CD 2-15

Facts about Earth's rotation

Speed	Direction	It decides
_____ km/h faster than the speed of _____	_____ to _____	distribution of deserts, _____ and _____

Scientists' simulation: changes on a backward-spinning Earth

Immediate effects	Future effects
• Trade winds would blow _____. • Hurricanes would travel from _____ to _____ across the Atlantic. • Westbound flights would be much _____ compared to eastbound ones.	• Because of changes in _____ patterns, the deserts in the world would _____ from _____ km² to _____ km². • More plants would _____ carbon dioxide. • Temperatures would drop by up to _____ Celsius.

 Reading

次の文を読んで、あとの問いに答えましょう。

DL 30   CD 2-16 ~ CD 2-20

online audio

Bright Half, Dark Half

The Earth's rotation dictates our daily lives. Namely, we are active during daylight hours and inactive during darkness. And whether standing on a street or lying in bed, we do not physically feel our planet's one-way revolving movement. However, if the Earth suddenly ground to a halt, we would be immediately aware
5 of the change no matter where we were or what we were doing.

With the Earth being completely still, the atmosphere surrounding the planet would continue to be in motion. In fact, the speed of one rotation would be around 1770 kilometers per hour. As a result, everything not firmly fixed to the planet's bedrock would be swept up and disappear into the atmosphere. This would include
10 not only buildings, people and animals, but also rocks, trees and even soil.

However, the likelihood of such a catastrophe occurring is virtually zero during the next few billion years. The explanation can be found in the fact that objects which are in motion tend to stay that way unless an outside force causes them to slow down. In the case of the Earth, there is almost nothing that stops it from continuing to spin. Yet, there are two factors that have affected its speed.

First, the collision that created the Moon added energy to our planet's rotational movement, which made a day on Earth just five hours long. Second, the Sun's gravitational pull has played a limited role in reducing the speed. But more importantly, tides raised by the force of gravity between the Moon and the Earth have slowed the latter's rotation to its present one day of 24 hours.

Scientists have actually measured and calculated that the gravitational effects of the Sun and Moon are slowing the spinning of the Earth by around 2 milliseconds every century. If such a scenario continues, at some point our planet will spin only once every 365 days, and this will lead to every spot on the planet having either permanent daytime or night-time. So, if humans are still inhabiting the planet at that point in time, we might all be living on its bright side.   (354 words)

1. What change would we experience if the Earth suddenly stopped?

    a. The Sun's gravity would directly affect anything on Earth.

    b. Things that are firmly fixed to the planet's bedrock would be blown away.

    c. We would have a catastrophe where everything on Earth's surface was gone.

    d. We would notice where we are at any time.

2. What is the most significant factor that decides the length of Earth's single rotation as 24 hours?

    a. forces of gravity we receive from other planets

    b. the atmosphere surrounding our planet

    c. the energy from the Moon to the Earth

    d. tides raised by the force of gravity between the Moon and Earth

3. Why can we say that the Earth will not suddenly stop in the next few billion years?

_____

_____

4. What factors have affected the speed of Earth's rotation?

_____

5. If the Earth's rotation speed slows down two milliseconds every century, what will happen to our planet?

_____

_____

✍ Writing

ブラジル人の友人 Pedro から「もしブラジルが夜の間に地球の自転がストップしたら、反対側の日本では何が起こる?」と聞かれました。ものが破壊されなかったという前提で起こりそうなことを3つ挙げて、Pedro へのメールを完成させましょう。

(起こりそうなこと)

1.	2.	3.

Hi Pedro,

If the Earth really stopped spinning, and it was daytime in Japan, first, _____

_____. Then, _____

_____. So if the Earth never started

rotating again, _____ in the end.

   Wow, this is just a kind of scary scenario, so let's hope it never actually

happens.

👉 Useful Expressions 「〜が起こるかもしれない、という表現」

Let me imagine that ... / What if ..., / Supposing ... / Let me take a hypothetical case.

🔊 Speaking and Discussion 🎧 DL 31 💿 CD 2-21 (online/audio)

次の Carol と Daisuke の会話を聞いて内容を理解しましょう。その後ペアを組み、各自 Carol と Daisuke になって Useful Expressions を参考に、会話の続きをつくってみましょう。

Daisuke: Did you watch *the Superman* movie made in 1978? The last scene is very exciting because he reverses the Earth's rotation to save his girlfriend.

Carol: Yes, I saw it, but I thought the last scene was ridiculous. It was too unrealistic.

Daisuke: Hey, Superman is "super," so he can make every impossible situation possible.

Carol: In the movie, that's true. Even so, I don't understand why the director ended the movie that way. It's a little childish.

Daisuke: Didn't you enjoy the movie at all, then?

· ↓続き↓ ·

Carol: Well, I enjoyed the story itself. I found it _____
_____.

Daisuke: So, you just didn't like the last scene.

Carol: That's right. As I told you, _____
_____.

Daisuke: _____.

👉 Useful Expressions

「ものごとの感想を尋ねる表現」
Did you like it(that)? / Did you enjoy …? / What did you think about …?
Did you find it …?

「感想を語る表現」
I found it / It was enjoyable (interesting / boring / exciting / awful).

UNIT 11
Silence Is Golden!

 **Warm-Up**

映像の写真をヒントに内容を予測して、次の質問に英語で答えましょう。

1.  *What are some causes of noise in big cities like New York and Tokyo?*

....

....

2. *What problems does noise cause?*

....

....

 **Video-Viewing 1**

online video   online audio

DL 32   CD 2-22

ビデオを見て、各キーワードを映像が出てくる順序に並べた場合、空所に入るものを
a〜eから選んでみましょう（1つ不要な選択肢があります）。

What was shown in a survey by the U.S. Census Bureau

(¹　　　)

An expert's opinion about noise pollution

(²　　　)

(³　　　)

(⁴　　　)

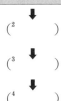

a. The results of a 1974 survey on noise pollution

b. The results of a 2007 survey on noise pollution

c. Problems caused by hearing loss

d. The reality and problems of noise pollution

e. Some countermeasures to noise pollution

▶◢ Video-Viewing 2

以下は映像の内容をまとめたものです。
空所に適語を入れましょう。

Noise Pollution in Big Cities

- No. 1 complaint is about _____ in the U.S.
- In the U.S., the background noise level is between ____ and ____ decibels (dB).

Health Problems (according to the WHO)

- Noise can cause long-term health problems such as _____ _____, _____ _____, and poor _____ and _____ performance.

Various Countermeasures to Noise Problems

Inexpensive earplugs	An easy, _____ fix
Implementing _____ hours	A more _____ solution Various cities have started
Ticketing people for noise pollution	In Germany, they banned _____ on Sundays. In Europe, they put noise restrictions on _____ products like _____, refrigerators and other household items. _____ has now banned the _____ gas engine.

📖 Reading

次の文を読んで、あとの問いに答えましょう。   🎧 DL 33   ◉ CD 2-23 ~ ◉ CD 2-26

Our Constant Companion

In this day and age of ever-advancing technology, sound is our constant companion. In almost every second of our daily lives it infiltrates us psychologically and can affect us physically. Surrounded by noise-making devices—both large and small—the most common example in modern society is undoubtedly the ubiquitous
5 smartphone. However, apart from enabling written communication, it would be nothing without its key feature—the ability to transfer sound.

A simple scientific explanation of sound would state it is "the energy produced by vibrations that travel in air or through objects, and into our ears and brains, where it is interpreted as noise, speech and music, etc." In other words, when you hear
10 a noise, you are listening to energy making a journey, and it can be imagined as waves travelling over the sea. At the start of the journey, the energy level is high,

but as it travels, it loses that energy. This explains why we hear less of a sound the further away we are from it.

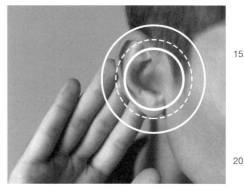

15

In air, sound travels at around 332 meters per second, which is far slower than the 300,000 kilometers per second for light. However, unlike light, sound can travel well through objects. And compared with moving in air, sound waves travel faster and

20

more effectively in liquids, and even more effectively in solids, which may seem to contradict popular belief. However, it is scientifically proven. In fact, sound is able to travel through water at roughly 1,500 meters per second, and approximately four times this figure in some solids.

25

The reason for the differences in speed is due to the level of molecule density. In a gas, for instance, molecules are loosely packed together. But in a liquid, they are more tightly packed, although not as tightly as in solids. Thus, the molecules in solids pass on the vibrating effects of a sound to each other more easily since they are in closer proximity. Perhaps you have already experienced this phenomenon 30 in elementary school when you made a simple telephone with two paper cups and some string: do you remember what sound you first made or heard?　　(355 words)

1. How fast can sound travel in solids?
　a. roughly 1,500 meters per second
　b. around 332 meters per second
　c. over 300,000 kilometers per second
　d. about 6 kilometers per second

2. What decides the speed of sound in various atmospheres and objects?
　a. the frequency of vibration in the air
　b. the density of the molecules in an object
　c. the quantity of the sound sources in the surroundings
　d. the tone of the sound in different places

3. According to the passage, what is the crucial function of a smartphone?

_____

_____

4. How can we scientifically define sound?

_____

_____

5. What does the underlined phrase "this phenomenon" refer to?

_____

_____

✍ Writing

スウェーデン人の Olga から「リラックスしたいときに聴くとよい効果音は何か」と聞かれました。薦めたい効果音を 3 つ挙げて、Olga へのメールを完成させましょう。

（薦めたい効果音）

1. [   ] **2.** [   ] **3.** [   ]

Dear Olga,

My first piece of advice is to listen to _____.

Just try to imagine _____. Also, it

might be a good idea to choose _____, such as _____

_____. It is so _____! And I

would recommend _____, too. They will

help you to relax at bedtime. I hope this advice is helpful.

Have a good sleep.

👉 **Useful Expressions「提案する、アドバイスを与える（応用編）」**

My first piece of advice is ... / It might be a good idea to ... / I would recommend you to ...
Let me tell you ...

📢 Speaking and Discussion 🎧 DL 34 ◉ CD 2-27 online audio

Akira と隣りに住む Ami の会話を聞いて内容を理解しましょう。その後ペアを組み、各自 Akira と Ami になって Useful Expressions を参考に、会話の続きをつくってみましょう。

Ami: Excuse me, I'm Ami, your next-door neighbor. Can I talk to you for a minute?

Akira: Oh, hi, Ami. We haven't met before. I'm Akira. Nice to meet you. What can I do for you?

Ami: Sorry to say this, but you've been making a lot of noise all day long today.

Akira: Oh, have I?　Is it disturbing you?

Ami: Yes, actually, the bell of your alarm clock was quite loud this morning. I could hear it clearly.

・・・・・・・・・・・・・・・・・・・・・・・・ ↓続き↓ ・・・・・・・・・・・・・・・・・・・・・・・・・・

Akira: I'm sorry about that. _____

_____ .

Ami: And I also heard _____ .

Akira: _____ .

Ami: _____ .

👉 **Useful Expressions**

「謝罪する際の表現」

I'm (terribly, awfully, very) sorry about (for) ... / Please accept my apologies about (for) ...
I do (must) apologize about (for) ... / I can't tell you how sorry I am about (for) ...

UNIT 12
What Is Your Type?

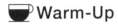Warm-Up

映像の写真をヒントに内容を予測して、次の質問に英語で答えましょう。

1.

What blood types do people have in the world?

....

....

2.

Why can't some blood types be mixed with other types?

....

....

 Video-Viewing 1

DL 35   CD 2-28

ビデオを見て、各キーワードを映像が出てくる順序に並べた場合、空所に入るものを
a ～ e から選んでみましょう（1つ不要な選択肢があります）。

A short history of research on blood type

(^{1})

How your blood plasma reacts to something foreign

(^{2})

(^{3})

The blood types of animals

(^{4})

a. Blood types of famous people in the world

b. What decides a blood type

c. The blood types valuable to certain diseases

d. Blood types in the world

e. Serious outcomes caused by the body's self-defense system

▶️ Video-Viewing 2

online video online audio

以下は映像の内容をまとめたものです。
空所に適語を入れましょう。

🎧 DL 35 ・◎ CD 2-28

How your blood reacts to a different type of blood

· Your blood has _____ called antigens. Each blood type has unique antigens.

· When a different type of antigen enters your body, the _____ in your blood plasma _____ themselves to the antigens.

· Your blood has _____ .

· They clog blood _____ , and blood circulation is disrupted.

8 dominant blood types = ___ , ___ , ___ , ___ , ___ , ___ , ___ , ___

Animals that have blood types

dogs cats _____ _____

📖 Reading

次の文を読んで、あとの問いに答えましょう。 🎧 DL 36 ◎ CD 2-29 ~ ◎ CD 2-34

online audio

Artificial Blood

It is generally known that if a patient is injected with blood that does not match his or her blood type, it might cause the individual severe problems, even death. But what if there was blood that could be used for anyone? If it did exist, it would be a medical miracle that could save many lives.

5 The good news is that Japanese researchers have reported success in developing artificial blood that can be transfused into patients regardless of their blood type. The blood was created by scientists from the National Defense Medical College, and they tested its effectiveness on ten rabbits suffering from severe blood loss. After injecting the artificial blood into the rabbits, the researchers found that six
10 survived without any adverse side effects, such as blood clotting.

As for people, when we actually need a typical blood transfusion, great caution must be exercised. Critically, the person's blood type must be identified before going ahead with the treatment. This is why emergency medical technicians and other healthcare workers are prohibited from transfusing blood in ambulances, which results in a loss of valuable time for patients.

15

20

   Time is also problematic in terms of storing real blood from donors. For example, blood platelets, which stop bleeding, can be stored for only four days. As for red blood cells, which carry oxygen to body cells, the situation is slightly better as they can be kept for 20 days at low temperatures.

   In contrast, the Japanese team's artificial blood consists of both platelets and red 25 blood cells that can be stored at normal temperatures for over a year. Moreover, since blood type is not an issue when injured patients receive the artificial blood, they can be treated before arriving at hospitals in the ambulance or even on the street.

   Commenting on this 'medical miracle,' one team member, Manabu Kinoshita, an 30 associate professor of immunology at the Medical College said, "It is difficult to stock a sufficient amount of blood for transfusions in such regions as remote islands," so "The artificial blood will be able to save the lives of people who otherwise could not be saved." (354 words)

1. Which component in blood stops bleeding?
   a. blood platelets
   b. blood plasma
   c. red blood cells
   d. white blood cells

2. What did the researchers find in the experiment with the rabbits?
   a. Artificial blood can be stored longer than natural blood.
   b. Artificial blood can carry more oxygen than natural blood.
   c. Artificial blood didn't cause negative side effects in some rabbits.
   d. Artificial blood worked well for all the animal subjects.

3. How long is it possible to keep the artificial blood the researchers developed?

_____

_____

4. Why are emergency medical technicians not allowed to transfuse blood in ambulances?

_____

_____

5. Why is artificial blood beneficial, especially for people living in remote areas?

_____

_____

✍ Writing

オランダ人の Eva から、血液型が B 型のボーイフレンドについて相談を受けました。彼女の国では血液型占いはほとんど知られていません。B 型の人の性格の好ましい点と好ましくない点を 2 つずつ挙げて、Eva へのメールを完成させましょう。

(好ましい点) (好ましくない点)

1. _____ 2. _____ 1. _____ 2. _____

_____ _____

Dear Eva,

First of all, a man with type B blood _____, which is just right for you because you always love doing something new. Also, he _____

_____, so he will tell you his true feelings. On the other hand, he can _____ because he likes keeping to his own pace. Also, he might _____ because of his changeable mood. The best match for a man with blood type B is a woman with type O, followed by a woman with type B. What is your blood type?

👉 Useful Expressions 「人の性格を表す形容詞」

adventurous / inconsistent / honest / good-natured / lazy / reckless / reserved / self-conscious selfish / straightforward

🔊 Speaking and Discussion 🎧 DL 37 💿 CD 2-35 (online audio)

次の Akira と Becky の会話を聞いて内容を理解しましょう。その後ペアを組み、各自 Akira と Becky になって Useful Expressions を参考に、会話の続きをつくってみましょう。

Akira: Becky! Where are you going? You look like you're in a great hurry.

Becky: A blood donation vehicle is here on campus, and it's closing in a few minutes.

Akira: Are you going to donate blood? Why?

Becky: Why!? It's for people who need it, of course! You know, there're a lot of patients who need new blood for their medical treatment.

Akira: Yes, I know that, but putting a needle in your arm... just thinking about it is scary.

· ↓続き↓ ·

Becky: Hey, why don't you come with me? It will help a lot of people.

Akira: _____. I don't feel good now.

Becky: Really? You look all right to me. And _____,

so it's not a big deal at all.

Akira: _____.

👉 Useful Expressions

「誘いを断る表現」
I'm afraid I can't. / I'd like to, but... / I wish I could, but / I'd better not. / I'd rather not.
No, thanks. / No, I wouldn't. / Certainly not.

New Homes for Humans?

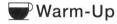 Warm-Up

映像の写真をヒントに内容を予測して、次の質問に英語で答えましょう。

1. *What is a super-Earth?*

Kepler 20b

GOLDILOCKS ZONE

....

....

2. *Can you imagine one advantage and one disadvantage of super-Earths?*

....

....

▶️ Video-Viewing 1

 online / video    online / audio

🎧 DL 38   ⦿ CD 2-36

ビデオを見て、各キーワードを映像が出てくる順序に並べた場合、空所に入るものを a ～ e から選んでみましょう（1つ不要な選択肢があります）。

Astronomers' findings about exoplanets

↓

(¹   )

↓

(²   )

↓

The effects of low gravity on a super-Earth planet

↓

(³   )

↓

(⁴   )

a. A possible problem of super-Earths

b. Super-Earth sizes and gravity

c. How spaceships must land on a super-Earth

d. The possible landscape on a super-Earth

e. What the Kepler Space Telescope discovered

▶◀ Video-Viewing 2

以下は映像の内容をまとめたものです。
空所に適語を入れましょう。

online / video　　online / audio

🎧 DL 38　💿 CD 2-36

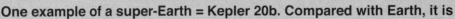

Facts about Super-Earths

- Among _____ exoplanets that the Kepler Space Telescope discovered, ____ % of them are super-Earths.

One example of a super-Earth = Kepler 20b. Compared with Earth, it is

- _____ the size
- _____ times more massive = gravity is almost _____ times stronger

Advantages	Disadvantages
• A _____ atmosphere is great for protection against harmful space _____.	• _____ Kepler 20b is extremely difficult. Compared to missions like the Apollo moon landings,
• Mountains and hills would _____ more quickly.	– it would require _____ the amount of fuel.
• "Just as _____ in Earth's oceans is richest in shallow waters near coastlines, such an 'archipelago world' might be enormously _____ to life." – René Heller	– rockets could only carry a _____ of the payload.

📖 Reading

次の文を読んで、あとの問いに答えましょう。　🎧 DL 39　💿 CD 2-37 ~ 💿 CD 2-40

online / audio

Hunting Hidden Planets

For centuries, human beings have gazed at the night sky wondering about the possibility of life on other planets, and whether there are some we might inhabit one day. And as time passes, the need to find a new home for the human race is becoming more important due to the depletion of Earth's limited resources and a
5　swelling global population.

In this quest, NASA began the Kepler Mission, whose goal was to survey an area of space containing around 150,000 stars like our Sun and detect planets for future human habitation. Suitable planets should be similar in size and possess features like those on Earth that could, in theory, support life. The Kepler spacecraft,
10　equipped with an ultra-sensitive telescope containing special detectors similar to

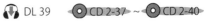

those found in digital cameras, surveyed stars in a region of the Milky Way closest to our present planet. In essence, the task represented a three-and-a-half-year space mission by an unmanned, planet-hunting observatory.

After its launch in March 6, 2009, the spacecraft soon started finding numerous small planets, indicating the Galaxy to be filled with more planets than stars. Among the planets, certain ones exhibited interesting features that amazed scientists. For instance, some orbit their parent star so closely that the surface facing the star is a fiery ocean of molten rock. Kepler's telescope also discovered planets that orbit not one but two stars, meaning that a dawn or dusk there shows two stars moving slowly across the sky.

Although it was expected to be in service for only a year, during its nine-year mission, Kepler discovered 2,682 possible candidate planets for human inhabitation. Included in the mass of data it sent back to Earth, nearly 2,100 more planets are still awaiting analysis. Among the already detected planets, one in particular is viewed as having excellent qualities for future settlement. Called Kepler-69c, its diameter is approximately 1.5 times larger than that of Earth. The only problem with this (and other potentially habitable planets) is distance—it's 2,700 light-years away. So even if we do find a suitable planet, how will we get there?

(348 words)

1. What was the mission of the Kepler spacecraft?

    a. to orbit stars with other planets

    b. to install ultra-sensitive telescopes on planets

    c. to gather data on potentially habitable planets

    d. to search for aliens in the Milky Way

2. Which finding from the Kepler Mission excited scientists?

    a. Kepler-69c rotates like the Earth.

    b. A limited number of stars exist in space.

    c. Some stars have more than one orbit.

    d. The surface of certain planets is not solid.

3. Why do we need to find a new home for the human race?

_____

_____

4. What can we expect when further analysis of the data from Kepler has been completed?

_____

_____

5. What is a major problem for us in going to Kepler-69c?

_____

_____

✍ Writing

Super-Earth の Kepler-69c に私たちのような人間がいたら、どのように地球や自分の国、自分自身の紹介をしますか? 紹介したいことを 3 つ挙げて、メールを完成させましょう。

（紹介したいこと）

1. [   ]　　**2.** [   ]　　**3.** [   ]

> Dear super-Earth friend,
>
>   Hello! I'm a human being on Earth, and I'd like to tell you about myself and my planet. First, let me introduce myself. My name is _____, and I'm _____.
>
> On Earth, _____ _____
>
> _____. My country, Japan, is _____
>
> _____.
>
> What kind of place do you live in? I'd really like to know more about you and your planet. I'm looking forward to hearing from you soon.

☛ Useful Expressions「自己紹介の表現」
May I introduce myself? / First, let me introduce myself …
Allow me to introduce myself …

📢 Speaking and Discussion DL 40  CD 2-41 (online audio)

次の Fumika と George の会話を聞いて内容を理解しましょう。その後ペアを組み、各自 Fumika と George になって Useful Expressions を参考に、会話の続きをつくってみましょう。

George: You know, people like us might be living on the super-Earth planet Kepler 20b in the future.

Fumika: Wow, that's an interesting idea! And maybe it will be possible for them to come and visit us—just like in that old movie *E.T.*

George: Yeah, maybe. But if someone, or an alien could come to Earth, where do you think they should go?

Fumika: To Japan, of course! I'd very much like them to enjoy the four seasons here.

George: Yes, Japan has a lot of charms in each season, but what in particular do you think they should do while they are here?

· ↓続き↓ ·

Fumika: Well, first of all, I think they should see _____

_____ .

George: _____ . Then what?

Fumika: _____ .

George: _____ .

👉 Useful Expressions

「招待する際の表現」

I'd very much like ~ to ... / I (We) would be very pleased if ~ could ...
I (We) should be delighted if ~ were able to (could) ...

UNIT 14
A New Life for Shells

 Warm-Up

映像の写真をヒントに内容を予測して、次の質問に英語で答えましょう。

1.
What things do you think can be made from lobster shells?

....

....

2.
How might lobster shells help solve environmental problems?

....

....

 Video-Viewing 1

 online video   online audio

DL 41   CD 2-42

ビデオを見て、各キーワードを映像が出てくる順序に並べた場合、空所に入るものを
a ～ e から選んでみましょう（1つ不要な選択肢があります）。

| The Shellworks and its members |
| ↓ |
| Crustacean waste and chitin |
| ↓ |
| (¹   ) |
| ↓ |
| (²   ) |
| ↓ |
| (³   ) |
| ↓ |
| An advantage and disadvantage of The Shellworks' current bioplastic |
| ↓ |
| (⁴   ) |

a. Bridging the gap between science and industry

b. Four machines and their purposes

c. How Shellworks make bio-plastics

d. Self-fertilizing plant pots

e. How to make waterproof bio-plastics

 Video-Viewing 2

以下は映像の内容をまとめたものです。
空所に適語を入れましょう。

online video   online audio

DL 41   CD 2-42

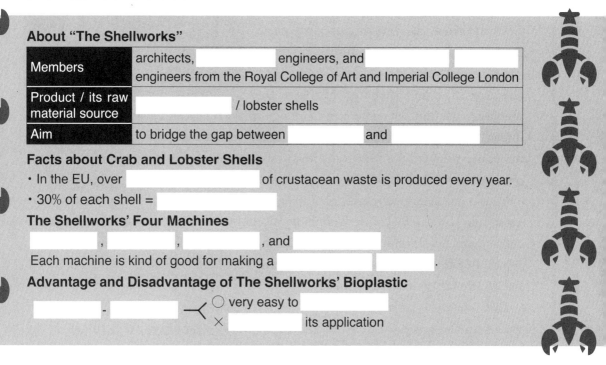

About "The Shellworks"

Members	architects, _____ engineers, and _____ _____ engineers from the Royal College of Art and Imperial College London
Product / its raw material source	_____ / lobster shells
Aim	to bridge the gap between _____ and _____

Facts about Crab and Lobster Shells

• In the EU, over _____ of crustacean waste is produced every year.

• 30% of each shell = _____

The Shellworks' Four Machines

_____, _____, _____, and _____

Each machine is kind of good for making a _____ _____.

Advantage and Disadvantage of The Shellworks' Bioplastic

_____ - _____ ⟨ ○ very easy to _____

× _____ its application

 Reading

次の文を読んで、あとの問いに答えましょう。   DL 42   CD 2-43 ~ CD 2-47

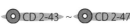

online audio

Precious Waste

A century ago, food was not abundant so the idea of losing or throwing away edible food would have seemed absurd. And for millions of people in poorer countries today, the idea is still unimaginable, with one in nine presently undernourished. However, in wealthy countries it is becoming a regular topic in
5 the news, since the issue primarily exists there.

Food loss and food waste are not exactly the same things. Food loss refers to the decrease in potentially-edible food when it is produced, harvested and processed. First, there is agricultural loss due to damage by mechanical machines when picking and sorting crops. Then, further loss occurs during handling, storage and
10 transportation from the farm to the various destinations for processing. There, the raw products are packed or canned, and spillage and damage cause further food

loss.

In contrast, food waste is when there is a loss of finished food products during the time of retailing and human consumption. For instance, a certain percentage of food is disposed of at wholesale markets, supermarkets and convenience stores. Yet, the area that gains most attention in the  15 media is consumption, and our tendency to throw away food unnecessarily. In 20 Japan, for example, it is estimated that 20 million tons of food is thrown away annually, although 9 million tons is still edible and within its consumption expiry date.

To combat this growing issue, Japan is taking action. For instance, steps are being taken to avoid overproduction of seasonal foods. Also, apps are being used to 25 sell shop and restaurant food that is nearing its sell-by date to consumers at lower prices. In addition, it has increased the number of food recycling banks across the nation to offer the food to the needy.

Even so, much more needs to be done to reduce the amount of edible food that goes into the trash, and the key is consumers everywhere, regardless of the 30 country. We must shop wisely and not think of food as a simple convenience that enables us to enjoy our daily lives. We have to think of food as if it were like the money we spend—precious.   (357 words)

1. How much food is thrown away with good reason annually in Japan?

   a. one million tons

   b. nine million tons

   c. eleven million tons

   d. twenty million tons

2. What is food loss?

   a. It is the habit of buying unnecessary food.

   b. It is the decrease in potentially edible food before it reaches shops.

   c. It is the disposal of food at both wholesale markets and retailers.

   d. It is a situation where many people are undernourished.

3. Why does agricultural loss occur?

_____

_____

4. What has Japan started doing to reduce the amount of food thrown away? Write three measures.

_____

_____

_____

5. What should consumers do to reduce food waste?

_____

_____

Writing

あなたは余剰食品リサイクル会社、Food Recyclers のサイトを閲覧し、何かを買いたいと思っています。買いたい食品を 3 つ挙げて、サイト宛てのメールを完成させましょう。

(買いたい食品)

1. [   ] 2. [   ] 3. [   ]

Dear Food Recyclers,

   I'm interested in the excess food you listed on your website. If it is still available, I would like to buy some. First, I want _____

_____ because I love the taste. What I need next is _____

_____ . Also, I'd love to get _____,

since _____. Please let me know if you still

have stocks of these items.

Thank you.

👉 Useful Expressions 「~ が欲しい、必要だという表現」

I need (want) ... / I'd like ... / I'd love to ... / What I need (want) is ...
Would it be possible for me to ...?

🔊 Speaking and Discussion 🎧 DL 43 💿 CD 2-48 (online audio)

次の Akira と Becky の会話を聞いて内容を理解しましょう。その後ペアを組み、各自 Akira と Becky になって Useful Expressions を参考に、会話の続きをつくってみましょう。

Akira: Look at this article! It says that these plastic items are made from crab shell.

Becky: Did you say "crab shell"?

Akira: Yes, the shells of crabs.

Becky: Their shells?

Akira: Yes, crustaceans have a hard shell, you know.

Becky: Sorry? I still don't really understand.

· · · · · · · · · · · · · ↓続き↓ · · · · · · · · · · · · · · ·

Akira: Well, _____.

Becky: _____.

Akira: _____.

Becky: _____.

👉 Useful Expressions

「相手の言ったことが分からなかった際の表現」
Sorry? / What? / What was that (again)?
I'm sorry I didn't catch (hear) ... / Did you say "..."?
Sorry, what did you say? / Could I ask you to repeat ...?

「言い換えをする際の表現」
In other words, / What I mean is ... / Let me put it another way:
All I'm trying to say is ...

Acknowledgements Original videos from INSIDER

Unit 1   How Contagious Is A Single Sneeze? (2018/11/2)
https://www.youtube.com/watch?v=MKAHNoni0KI

Unit 2   The Most Impressive Dads In The Animal Kingdom (2018/11/21)
https://www.youtube.com/watch?v=mN1J-Jeh_AA

Unit 3   How Eating Spicy Food Affects Your Brain And Body (2017/10/30)
https://www.youtube.com/watch?v=TuVcnR5zAWo&list=PL8WDfn06DASkowj9buUg7c6L2fxLZ
NatZ&index=27

Unit 4   What If All Insects Disappeared? (2019/9/1)
 https://www.youtube.com/watch?v=XjfbXU5nFS0

Unit 5   Here's why NASA spacesuits are white (2019/4/15)
https://www.insider.com/why-are-nasa-spacesuits-white-2019-4

Unit 6   What Humans Will Look Like In 1,000 Years (2017/5/6)
https://www.youtube.com/watch?v=BibBMBibTq0

Unit 7   What If All The Ice Melted Overnight (2019/10/4)
https://www.youtube.com/watch?v=EP97oqa9JJo&list=PL8WDfn06DASnCDU9EHnLcaTJ18iY
OCXS3&index=5&t=0s

Unit 8   Why 5 million Americans get their wisdom teeth removed each year (2018/10/19)
https://www.businessinsider.com/why-wisdom-teeth-suck-dentist-dental-health-2018-10

Unit 9   How Nonrecyclable Plastic Bags Are Being Turned Into Speakers (2019/5/3)
https://www.youtube.com/watch?v=-shSLvLOsoQ&list=PLxzJmNzonMVMtLW0z3E9bNNIWI_
RTv-sE&index=16

Unit 10   What If Earth Started Spinning Backwards? (2018/10/19)
https://www.youtube.com/watch?v=ilyLX9f4hY8

Unit 11   Noise Pollution Is Much Worse For You Than You Think (2018/1/25)
https://www.youtube.com/watch?v=5jfmzufa8qo&list=PLxzJmNzonMVMtLW0z3E9bNNIWI_
RTv-sE&index=37

Unit 12   Why You Can't Mix Blood Types (2018/7/5)
https://www.youtube.com/watch?v=fRB98GpELD4

Unit 13   Is There A Better Planet Out There For Us? (2018/7/1)
https://www.youtube.com/watch?v=UW1J5J-tzKw

Unit 14   How Lobster Shells Could Replace Single-Use Plastic (2019/4/29)
https://www.youtube.com/watch?v=wBSzxQLQSpI&list=PLxzJmNzonMVMtLW0z3E9bNNIWI_
RTv-sE&index=17

オンライン映像配信サービス「plus⁺Media」について

本テキストの映像と音声は plus⁺Media ページ（www.kinsei-do.co.jp/plusmedia）から、ストリーミング再生でご利用いただけます。手順は以下に従ってください。

ログイン

- ●ご利用には、ログインが必要です。
  サイトのログインページ（www.kinsei-do.co.jp/plusmedia/login）へ行き、plus⁺Media パスワード（次のページのシールをはがしたあとに印字されている数字とアルファベット）を入力します。

- ●パスワードは各テキストにつき１つです。
  有効期限は、<u>はじめてログインした時点から１年間</u>になります。

ログインページ

[利用方法]

次のページにある QR コード、もしくは plus⁺Media
トップページ（www.kinsei-do.co.jp/plusmedia）から該当するテキストを選んで、そのテキストのメインページにジャンプしてください。

メニューページ　　　再生画面

plus+Media トップ　　　メインページ

「Video」「Audio」をタッチすると、それぞれのメニューページにジャンプしますので、そこから該当する項目を選べば、ストリーミングが開始されます。

[推奨環境]

iOS (iPhone, iPad)	OS: iOS 6 〜 13 ブラウザ：標準ブラウザ	Android	OS: Android 4.x 〜 10.0 ブラウザ：標準ブラウザ、Chrome
PC	OS: Windows 7/8/8.1/10, MacOS X　ブラウザ: Internet Explorer 10/11, Microsoft Edge, Firefox 48以降, Chrome 53以降, Safari		

※最新の推奨環境についてはウェブサイトをご確認ください。
※上記の推奨環境を満たしている場合でも、機種によってはご利用いただけない場合もあります。また、推奨環境は技術動向等により変更される場合があります。予めご了承ください。

このシールをはがすと
plus+Media 利用のための
パスワードが
記載されています。

一度はがすと元に戻すことは
できませんのでご注意下さい。

◀ここからはがして下さい

4121
World Insiders

plus+Media

本書には音声 CD（別売）があります

World Insiders
–Authentic Videos from *INSIDER*
INSIDER で観て学ぶ 総合英語と世界の深部

2021年 1 月20日 初版第 1 刷発行
2022年 2 月20日 初版第 3 刷発行

編著者　　　吉 田 国 子
　　　　　　Anthony Allan

発行者　　　福 岡 正 人
発行所　　株式会社　金 星 堂
（〒101-0051）東京都千代田区神田神保町 3-21
Tel. (03) 3263-3828 （営業部）
　　 (03) 3263-3997 （編集部）
Fax (03) 3263-0716
http://www.kinsei-do.co.jp

編集担当　長島吉成　　　　　　　　　Printed in Japan
印刷所・製本所／三美印刷株式会社

ISBN978-4-7647-4121-8　C1082